BOUNCE BACK and Thrive

Skills for Resilience
Jeff Vankooten

Published by WRC^2 Media

WRC2Media.com

For ordering information or special discounts for bulk purchases, contact info@WRC2Media.com.

Written by Jeff Vankooten

Edited by Kris Harty

Cover Design by Wes Connell

ISBN 978-0-692-83474-9

Thank you!

I want to thank three amazing people in my life specifically for this simple book - Kris Harty, Wayne Connell, and Wes Connell

Kris Harty masterfully edited the manuscript. Kris Harty speaks, edits, and inspires (a real renaissance woman).

Wayne Connell enthusiastically did the publishing grunt work.

Wes Connell beautifully designed the cover

Thank you all... A guy like me couldn't do this without people like **YOU!**

A merchant ship loaded with gold, silver, and other precious jewels was on its way back to port when it was suddenly confronted by a pirate ship. Seeing their turrets ablaze and the skull and crossbones flags flapping in the wind, the excitable first mate asked the captain what they should do.

The captain replied, "First mate, go into my war chest and bring me my red shirt."

The captain, after donning that red shirt, was an inspiration to his men, and they repelled that pirate ship without any casualties.

A couple days went by, and the merchant ship was again confronted by three pirate ships. The excitable first mate again asked, "Captain, what should we do?"

The captain responded, "First mate, go into my war chest and bring me my red shirt."

Upon wearing that red shirt, the captain was again an inspiration for his men. They fought valiantly for him, and they repelled those three pirate ships, with hardly any casualties.

That night as they were celebrating their victory, the first mate asked, "Captain, what's the secret to the red shirt?"

The captain confidently stated, "It's simple, really. It's red because red won't show the red from my bloodied wounds, and that will inspire the men to continue to fight for me valiantly and bravely."

A few more days went by, and this time, the merchant ship was confronted by 10 pirate ships.

The first mate excitedly asked, "Captain, should I get you your red shirt?"

The captain thought for one brief second. "First mate, go into my war chest and bring me my brown pants."

Most of us might not have pirate ships to contend with in our daily lives. But most of us can relate to the need for brown pants to face the chaos and uncertainty of our challenging days.

There are many opportunities today to wear our brown pants. Look around you: there are brown pants everywhere.

There are brown pants being worn in families, there are brown pants being worn in workplaces. There are brown pants being worn around the world. People are fearful about all the changes that are happening, all the massive changes that are going on.

If we had to summarize these three changes, if there were three pirate ships, if you will, that seemed to be driving most of the brown pants, it would be these three:

An uncertain global economic outlook: You could also say an uncertain personal economic outlook. If you look around the world, it seems as if the economy is a huge weight on so many people, countries, continents and the debt that our own country and citizens hold here. These economic uncertainties cause us to wear our brown pants.

New Technology: Another pirate ship that seems to hold us in fear is the rapid availability of, and the penetration of, new technology. Technology is a great thing, but everything is a two-sided coin. Think about technology today. The smartphone has more computing power than NASA had available to get men to the moon. We now have biotechnology and nanobots. What does it mean to be human with all of this technology?

A lot of people today worry about our present culture: have we caught up with the ramifications of all the technology that is coming our way? We wear our brown pants.

Shorter and Faster Business Cycles: We can become professionally irrelevant quickly. Many people are scared about that possibility. College graduates can earn degrees in a field that has them applying for jobs that don't exist yet. Changes are happening so quickly; it causes us to wear our brown pants.

If you've been to an optometrist, you've experienced the contraption placed on your face. The optometrist begins to calibrate. The doctor clicks once to see what the tension point is for your eye. He or she has you look at one dot. You look at that one dot, and then you hear click and click, and you're told to say when you see two dots. Then there are suddenly two dots, and the doctor has calculated the tension point in your eye from one dot to two dots.

We live in that tension point right now. There was the world that we knew: we were oriented, it was settled, it seemed like a safe place, but now there's a world that's emerging of a new orientation. We're not quite sure how we're going to live there. We wear our brown pants We are smack dab in the middle of this tension between then and what's coming up in the future. We often want to retreat to what is familiar, retreat to the world that is passing and is not coming back.

We can react to these fears, our modern-day pirate ships, in several ways, brown pants notwithstanding.

One of the most common and easiest ways to react is to retreat. We turn around. We have our tails between our legs. We whimper ourselves back to where we were in the first place, and we simply retreat.

We can also react by resisting. We can grit our teeth and resist the changes that are coming our way.

I think of my grandfather. He hurt his neck quite badly and he went to the doctor, and the doctor would turn his head away using his hand. The doctor asks, "Does that hurt?" "No." He'd do it again, "No." He was resisting. He was a tough-as-nails guy, so he didn't want to admit that he was hurting.

It's the same way with some of us as we try to respond to changes and to these marauders that are coming down upon us. We resist, "Is the change bothering you?" "No." "Is the change going to be big for you?" "No."

We resist. That's not the best response.

We also might react by simply resigning. We throw in the towel. We put up the white flag. There's nothing I can do, you say, so I'm going to lay down on the battlefield. The change and the pirates, whatever is coming, they're going to have to do what they're going to do because I have no way to know how to handle this and I don't have the strength. I'm going to resign as I respond to change in my life.

We can also retrench as a reaction. We can grit our teeth. We can hunker down. We can go back and trench ourselves against the changes that are coming. World War I showed us that trench warfare doesn't work. To retrench against the changes is not a good response either.

The best response to the changes that we are experiencing today, to the pirates that are coming down upon us on this sea of change, is to resile. Don't resign, don't retrench, don't retreat, instead resile.

Merrian Webster says that resile is a resilient word; it's been around in English since at least 1529. It's also a cousin of "resilient" - both words derive from the Latin verb resilire, "which means to jump back" or "recoil." Resilience is that ability, the innate ability, to persist and thrive in disruption, setbacks and change.

Resilience isn't something that some people have and other people don't have. Maybe you've thought that some people are much more resilient, and you don't have resilience. That's not true. It's what Anne Maston calls "ordinary magic".

Is your thinking something like this? "Change really does a whole big number on me. It's a big bad world, and I can't handle it."

But resilience is innate. Every single person has resilience within them. This isn't something that you're either gifted with or you're not. It's a matter of building skills, a skill base, to help you be more resilient as you engage the changes in your life.

Wheel of Resilience

You can respond with resilience. You can persist, you can thrive in disruption, setbacks and change. That's an incredible thing to know.

There are skills that you can master to help you be more resilient. Those are the skills we're going to look at here.

At the back of this book is a diagram of the **Wheel of Resilience**. Keep your finger on it as we go through this next section.

These resilience factors have been formulated through social sciences and psychology as to what makes people and organizations and communities thrive in disruption and change.

Rate yourself on where you believe you're at with each of these skills at this time. A rating of one is the lowest and four is the highest.

If you are open to change, and I'll explain what that means in a minute, you would have a line up to four. If you feel like you're not all that open to change, then you would have a two or even a one, and that's ok at this point. At the end of the chapter, you'll be able to see and graph what your resilience quotient is after reading more on the topic.

Refer to the **Wheel of Resilience** as I share about these different skills. See where you rate low and what type of effort you might need to increase your resilience around each of these particular skills.

Resilience Skill 1: Be Ready Not to Be Ready (Be Open)

The first skill is to be ready not to be ready. That sounds like something that was conjured up over about three or four pints of beer in a pub.

I can remember when my first born came into the world. We waited the usual nine months, of course, and when the due date came and went, we waited another three weeks.

Finally, we put ourselves into the delivery room in the hospital. My wife was in labor for 33 hours!

I watched David Letterman three times, waiting for this baby to come. And yes, I had the easy end of that deal.

If you've been in a modern delivery room, you know they're nicer than your bedroom. They have beautiful walls and comfortable couches. When the baby is ready to come, the room becomes like a transformer.

The walls open up, things fall down, lights turn on. The nurses come in with their booties already on their shoes, ready to work.

I was so excited. I was 'down there' in baseball like a catcher. I was ready to have this baby come into the world (not as ready as my wife was), and I was coaching her with the breathing technique we'd learned: "One breath, honey, two breaths, one breath, two two one one."

Finally, after waiting this long, the baby came. It was a son. We had a child, we had a son.

I'll never forget, they put that child, my boy, into my arms, and I looked at him, and the first thing I thought was, "Ewww."

I thought, I am so good looking (ok, tongue in cheek), how can my baby be so ugly?

He had been in amniotic fluid for almost 10 months. His eyes looked like afterthoughts. I wasn't ready. I read the book "What to Expect When You're Expecting," but I wasn't expecting that.

I learned as a parent right away, to be ready not to be ready.

We have to realize that we're not going to get what we expect most of the time.

In order to be resilient, and engage the marauders of change, whether globally or personally in our lives, we need to be ready not to be ready.

The way to be ready not to be ready is to have some contingency plans.

Having contingency plans in place are something to fall back on when things become unexpected in your life.

The first contingency plan is to learn is to embrace chaos. Yes, embrace chaos.

If you were living in the late '60s and early '70s, you knew a television show called Get Smart. Remember Get Smart, with Maxwell Smart and the shoe phone?

In the late '60s and early '70s, our culture and our country were going through a lot. There was the Vietnam war and there was Watergate. So many things were tumultuous in our society, and here comes this show Get Smart.

The enemy organization that Maxwell Smart was committed and devoted to defeating was Chaos. The heroic organization, the organization that was going to win the day that he worked for was called Control.

Here we were, living in a time of chaos, where we felt we had to get control back, at least that's what we thought. Just like Maxwell Smart, a bumbling spy, we didn't know quite how to get control, but we were going to bumble our way through it. Make no mistake, we humans have to have control. Or so we think.

Social scientists, those who tickle, poke and prod us to see how we function, say that we live under what's called the illusion of control.

This illusion of control helps us get by now and again, but we live by what we think is control, which is really only an illusion.

We do it every day. Think about going to get on an elevator. We push the light and it's activated and it lights up. If we're in a hurry or it doesn't come on our time schedule, what do we do? We push it again, as if we can control this huge contraption.

The area of my biggest illusion of control is traffic jams. I play traffic jams like chess games. I always pick a car by the make or the color, and that car is going to be my competitor.

I make my moves. I try to get past them. I look and I make the move and I see the car that I'm coming up against, and I pass him and I wave as I go by. He's not even playing the game. I'm going along and all of a sudden, here comes my competitor coming behind me, and he passes me.

When it all is said and done, I realize I had no control at all over how traffic moved or allowed me to move. I thought that I did, but it was just the illusion of control.

Once we realize control is an illusion, it can help us catch a deep breath to say, "Okay," I need to embrace chaos. Chaos is really the rule of the day for the most part, and that's one way for me to be more resilient.

It's a contingency plan of embracing chaos that helps us to be ready not to be ready.

The second contingency plan to be ready not to be ready is to enact a bad plan. Hear me out.

Every plan that you have is a bad one. It is. You can't wait until all the lights are green to take a trip. If you had a plan that was so meticulous and so planned out and so perfect, you'd be waiting forever because that's never going to happen.

You go with the plan that you have. When I think about my wife and me in our parenting, we have a bad plan. It's a bad plan that comes up every week. It's the only plan that we have, and so we go with it.

In fact, World War II and D-Day, that was a bad plan. You talk to the planners and they will tell you, it didn't go according to their plan. It was a bad plan, but it was the only plan they had, so they went with it.

Think about the plans that you have for your life. Think about the plans that you have for your children. Think about the plans you have for your career. They're bad.

Settle in on the fact that they're bad plans, because what you need to do is know where you are, where you want to go, and then what's the next step to get there. That is the plan.

Then you adjust and take soundings as you go, and you'll realize that there isn't a straight line from where you are to where you want to be. It is a wandering, meandering line as you go through, following this bad plan, but it gets you there, and you learn something wonderful.

In fact, if you enact a bad plan, you allow serendipity to take over. Serendipity's a wonderful thing. It's these unplanned little joys that come into our lives, that if we plan so meticulously, we would miss.

Intellectual serendipity leads to revelation. Spiritual serendipity leads to mystery. Relational serendipity often leads to romance and occupational serendipity often leads to our destiny.

Wanting to know precisely where we are going, is often how we fail to go anywhere at all.

Look at the **Wheel of Resilience** again.

How open are you to change?

How open are you to the unexpected?

How open are you to operate via a bad plan?

Are you open to letting things happen?

Are you open to serendipity?

Are you open to surprise and chaos?

How open are you to dealing with the changes that come your way?

Resilience Skill 2: Make Full Use of the Present (Be Committed)

The next resilience skill to help us engage and confront the marauders of change that come our way is to make full use of the present.

Make full use of the present.

In the movie, City Slickers, the character played by Billy Crystal is experiencing a midlife crisis. He is in angst about his life. He has turned 40 and he's wondering what in the world everything is about, and he's having this midlife crisis. He sells airtime for advertising on a radio station.

His son invites his dad to come to his fifth-grade career day to share with the class what he does. But before his dad comes to class, his son researches what exactly his dad does for a living. He decides it's not very exciting.

So while Billy Crystal's character is in the midst of a midlife crisis and wrestling with the meaning of it all, including who he is and what he does for work, he and his son are in the classroom with these fifth graders, and his son gets up and introduces his dad.

"I want you to meet my dad. He's a submarine commander."

That's the last straw for poor Billy Crystal.

Here is what he tells you, the fifth-grade class. This is his litany.

"Value this time in your life, kids, because this is the time in your life when you still have your choices and it goes by so fast. When you're a teenager, you think you can do anything, and you do. Your 20s are a blur. Your 30s, you start a family, you make a little money, and you think you're so, 'What happened to my 20s?' Your 40s, you grow a little belly, you grow another chin. A girlfriend from high school becomes a grandmother and the music starts to get too loud. The 50s, you'll have a surgery. You'll call it a procedure, but it's a surgery. The 60s, the music's still too loud but it doesn't matter because you can't hear it anyway.

"The 70s, you and the missus retire to Florida where you start having dinner at two in the afternoon, lunch at 10 in the morning, breakfast the night before. You wander the malls looking for the ultimate in soft yogurt, muttering to yourself, 'How come the kids don't call?" Your 80s, you'll have a massive stroke and you'll end up babbling to some Jamaican nurse whom your wife can't stand but whom you call mama. Any questions?"

I have not found anywhere a better description of the challenges and the swiftness of life than that litany from Billy Crystal in the movie City Slickers.

If we realize how life goes, we can make full use of the present, because every moment matters.

There are certain things we can do to help us become more resilient and to make full use of the present.

One thing we can do is understand the <u>dynamics of time</u>. The first dynamic about time is, it's short.

I don't have to describe this to anybody, we're always talking about 'boy, how time flies,' or 'I can't believe how it seems like it was just yesterday.' I've never heard anyone say, "Its taken a long time to grow old."

We use language frequently to describe how short time is.

Think about it.

Scientists estimate that humans have been around for 200,000 years.

The average lifespan for a North American is 78 years.

In the perspective of a 200,000 human existence, a 78 year life is the equivalent to 13 seconds.

Each second corresponds to six years.

How do we spend those 13 seconds?

One of the major activities we engage in is sleep.

We sleep from the moment we come into the world. We average about eight hours every night until we leave this planet at about age 78.

That amounts to 24 years that we spend sleeping.

We have to knock off four seconds of a 13 second life for sleep.

We work. That's another major activity that utilizes our time.

Someone who starts working at age 18, retires at age 65, and worked 40 hours a week, 50 weeks a year with two weeks off for vacation, their work time comes up to about 18 years.

We wait a lot, too. We're in our cars and in traffic a lot, what amounts to two seconds in our universe's long timeline. "We watch screens and other forms of entertainment for 18 years. That is another 3 seconds taken off our time line."

When push comes to shove, there's one second left.

We have one second left in our lives, beyond the sleeping, beyond the working, beyond the entertaining ourselves, beyond the waiting and other sundry activities that we involve ourselves in.

How are we spending that one last second?

What are we doing to make a difference in the world? What are you doing to make the most of that second that we have on this planet, and to be resilient so we can make the most of the situations that come our way? What are we doing to really live life at every turn, to make full use of the present?

When we realize how short time is, we're more apt to live more fully.

Life is short, time is short.

The second dynamic of time is that it's incredibly valuable.

Everybody has the same amount of time. The president of the United States, the most powerful person in the country, has as much time to use as you and I do. The president has no special dispensation to get more time into his life.

We all have the same amount of time, and it is valuable. That one second is valuable.

Let's say someone puts into your bank account every single day, $86,400. The contingency is, you must spend all of it in one day. Every day, you must spend what they put into your bank, $86,400, and it doesn't accrue. Whatever you don't spend, you lose.

That's the same gift that we're getting every day in our lives. We're given 86,400 seconds of each day.

How are we spending those 86,400 seconds we're given each day?

How are we investing our 86,400 seconds so we can make the most of it in our relationships, in our jobs, whatever it might be that we consider valuable?

To live fully in the present means that we are intentionally committed to the time that we're given.

Commitment is a big part of using our time intentionally.

How committed are you to making the most of the time that you have?

A friend of mine who teaches at the University of Denver gave me this definition of commitment, and I've not heard anything better.

He defined commitment as making the choice to give up choices.

Making the choice to give up choices, because choices come at us fast and furious.

When you think about your time, the dynamics of it, that it's short and it's valuable, are you open to making the choice to give up the other choices?

How committed are you to making full use of the present? Mark it on the **Wheel of Resilience**.

Resilience Skill 3: Let Go of What's Going Away (Be Adventurous)

We need to be ready not to be ready. We need to make full use of the present. We also need to let go of what's going away.

I've had to let go of my hair. Back in the day, I had a nice wave in my hair. Now I have a beach. When I shaved my head, it saved a lot of barber costs.

You've got to let go of what's going away.

Do you have a bad habit in your life? Let it go.

Do you have a business plan that isn't working? Let it go.

Men, you replace your underwear once every eight years. That's the statistic. Men replace their underwear once every eight years. It makes sense.

I remember in college, I waited until mine were an elastic band with two flaps, front and back like Tarzan, before I replaced my underwear. Let it go. Get new underwear; let it go.

We need to let go of what's going away, and it's really, really tough.

I read an interesting article in the Wall Street Journal with the headline of "What is it about Toy Story 3 that makes grown men cry?"

I wanted to know more about the answer first-hand, so my wife and I watched the movie. It helped me understand what the article was saying. Andy, the star, the main character in all three of the Toy Story movies, was now a senior in high school. He was getting ready to go off to college. He had to figure out what to do with these toys that he was so endeared with most of his life, and he had to let them go.

I think for men, the movie was all about letting go of childish things, and there's a scene where Andy's mom is in Andy's room, and all the posters are off the wall, all the toys are packed up in boxes, the mattresses are off the bunk bed, and his room is as empty as can be.

There's his mom, standing in the midst of it. While we're watching this scene, I hear my wife next to me, sniffling. I look and she's crying. I started to cry, because I realized our son Josh is almost there. He's going to have his empty room before we know it this year, and he's going to be moving on.

For us to bounce back from his moving on, for us to persist and to thrive in the pain of that big move, we'll have to let him go. It'll be hard to do that.

We all know helicopter parents who are constantly in touch with their college kids. The parents are having a hard time letting go of their child, and letting their child grow up into adulthood in the way that he or she has to do. You've got to let them go. You've got to let go of what's going away.

We've got to let go of the past. We must let go of what's going away. Let go of the hope that you're going to have a better past. The past is not going to be any better than it was. It is what it is. Let go of what's going away.

Letting go involves <u>two strategies</u>.

One strategy of letting go is that you risk. If you want to let go of what's going away, you need to risk. We have what's called ambiguity aversion. We are fearful of risk, because we would rather stay in a situation that's known even though it's miserable, than take the risk into a future that's unknown but possibly much better. We often don't take the risk to move forward or to let anything go.

When deciding to risk or not, consider this statistic. Those who take great risks make two major mistakes a year. Those who don't take great risks make two major mistakes a year.

You're going to blow it, anyway, you might as well do it risking something that's really going to matter.
If there are five frogs on a log and one frog decides to jump off, how many frogs are left on the log? Five. There's a big difference between deciding to jump and jumping.

Don't decide to almost do something.

Do something and risk something that means something, that helps you let go of what's going away.

After that, the second strategy to letting go, is to intend to relax. Relax a little bit. We are the most keyed up country on the entire planet. Not only do you see brown pants everywhere, but you see teeth grinded down and jaw muscles working overtime every single day.

People are tense and uptight about everything that's going on in their lives and on the planet. You're not going to let anything go if you're holding it so tightly. You need to risk but you need to relax a little bit.

Open up to the surprises in life. Get yourself a glass of red wine tonight and hang out and watch something funny. Put your feet up onto the coffee table and catch your breath and relax.

Of the illnesses that are seen in doctors' offices, 90% are stress related illnesses. We as a country are so keyed up. You're not going to move forward unless you risk and relax.

Think about a trapeze. Life is often a series of trapezes. We go on one trapeze and we're swinging away and life seems exhilarating, and then as we look back, we realize, you know what, here's another trapeze that's empty.

You know that as you're swinging, you have to get on that other trapeze because that's how you're going to move ahead in your life, and the only way you're going to do that is if you make the decision to risk.

Say to yourself, "I'm going to do it, I'm really going to do it." Then relax enough to open your hands. Then boom, you take a risk, go over to the next trapeze, and life goes on again.

You've let go of what's going away and you've moved forward to where you need to go. That is one of the ways that you can become more resilient.

Be ready not to be ready. Make full use of the present. Let go of what's going away by risking and relaxing. You must let go to see if there was something worth holding on to.

How adventurous are you? How open to surprise? How much do you risk? What's your tolerance for risk? How well do you relax? Chart it on your **Wheel of Resilience**.

Resilience Skill 4: Take Time to Think (Be Focused)

Another resilience skill is to take time to think. There are things in life that if you ponder them long enough, make you scratch you head and say, "Hmm." Yes, things that make you go, "Hmm."

For instance, think about a hot water heater. Why do we need to heat hot water? Shouldn't it be a cold water heater? Hmm.

Think about the world of statistics. four out of five people suffer from diarrhea. Does that mean one of our five enjoys it? Hmm.

Think about boy's bicycles. Why? Why is the bar high on a boy's bicycle and low on a girl's? Hmm.

More seriously, there are many things in life that if we ponder them enough, they'll lead to new insights, new ways of seeing and viewing things.

We need to take time to think.

It's extremely hard in this day and age to take time to think because of our digital information age. Every year, Americans download from the blogosphere, from the atmosphere, from the digerati, from all the information that's coming our way, 3.6 zetabytes of information. That's as much information in a year than has ever been written or recorded in any book written in all of history.

All the information in every book that's ever been published, 3.6 zetabytes is more than that. If you Twittered 365 days a year every single second for 100 years, you would get close to 3.6 zetabytes of information.

As a society, we've become incredibly numb. It's called a "narcotizing dysfunction". We become immune to all the information. We become numb to the information that comes our way. We don't even know what to attend to. Our reaction is to stop and not take time to think anymore.

Not that long ago, 60 or 70 years ago, the primary ways of getting information were limited. There were family stories, the "I remember when" stories that your grandparents used to tell. There were schools, radio, newspapers, magazines, movies and neighbors. You would get your information primarily from those conduits.

Today, our information conduits are too many to list, and the list continues to grow.

In addition to all the older conduits mentioned above, we've added television, computers, pagers, cellphones, instant messaging, worldwide web, interweaving advertising, wireless communication, portal to entertainment blogs, global positioning, Twitter, video sharing, podcasts, video casts, streaming video, text message, online auctions, broadband, webisodes, satellites, pings, digital downloads, online gaming, and the list goes on and on and on.

That's how we've gotten to 3.6 zetabytes of information. After a while, we don't know what to do with all that information. We no longer care, because we're not taking the time to think any more about all the information that is coming at us.

We become resilient when we take time to think. It helps us in many ways.

Picture this. Your doorbell rings at one in the morning. You look through the peephole. You see a man who looks to be wealthy based on his clothing and appearance.

You're curious what this is about, so you open the door. He tells you that he's on a scavenger hunt with his wife.

The only item he needs for the scavenger hunt is a three foot by seven-foot piece of wood. If you get that for him, he'll give you $10,000.

You wrack your brain. You consider what's in the garage and if you have any piece of wood that's three foot by seven foot. After a mental check of what's in your garage, you conclude you don't have any such size wood.

You regretfully say, "I am so sorry, I wish I did because I could use $10,000, but I don't have such a piece of wood."

The next day as you're walking about your house, you stop dead in your tracks. It dawns on you that you have several pieces of wood that are three foot by seven foot.

Every door fits that description. Doors are everywhere. If only you'd had the insight to think beyond your first impulses and to look at the situation from a different perspective, you would've increased your bank account by $10,000.

Taking time to think helps us see and grasp ideas that we might have missed before.

Take time to think. You can do this by developing two mindful practices.

The first practice is contemplation. One of the main ingredients for contemplation is to be quiet.

In our busy lives, we need to take time to contemplate, and to be quiet.

I am going to give you a gift right now. I'm going to give you 30 seconds of silence: 30 seconds away from reading or doing anything else.

Let me give you 30 seconds, and I want you to think about what that feels like to have 30 seconds uninterrupted right now in your day. If you have a timer handy on your electronic device or anywhere else, I suggest you use it.

Go.

Thirty seconds of silence. No reading.

Stop.

I bet that felt good, didn't it? It may feel awkward at first, but once you get accustomed to it, it feels good to have quiet and silence.

To have mindful practices and become more resilient, we need to build silence into our lives.

Silence comes to us in our leisure time. Leisure time is when we can let our minds explore and think deeply.

The Greek root for school and scholarship is the word *schola. Schola* means leisure.

Leisure, but not in the sense of lying in a hammock with an umbrella drink, but leisure in the sense that you have unencumbered time to explore something deeply.

When I ask teachers if they believe their classroom is a place of schola, a place of leisure, they look at me like I'm nuts.

"Are you kidding me? I hardly have time to teach the subjects that I'm required to teach. Classroom time is not leisure time."

Think about your own life. Do you have leisure time built in to explore something that you're interested in? Do you have time set aside to ponder and wonder about life?

You know who does, and who does this well? Kids. We can learn how to wonder from the lives of children.

Children are amazing and can teach us much about how to live, if we let them.

For example, have you had a child come up to you and ask you to throw him up in the air?

When you do, what's the next thing he says? Do it again. Do it again, do it again, do it again. Soon, your arms get tired. "Do it again," you hear.

Kids delight in the monotonous.

They find wonder in the monotonous ways of life.

As we grow older, we lose that sense of wonder in our lives.

We lose a sense of knowing that the world holds wondrous things. We don't think about such things anymore.

We don't take the time to leisurely think about and contemplate the wonders of life.

It's a dangerous milestone when we stop wondering. When we lose the sense of wonder, we lose a sense of gratitude. We're no longer thankful for amazing things that come into our lives because we don't have a sense of wonder.

Here's an example of how wonder allows for gratitude to come into our lives.

Consider Captain Sully Sullenberger, the man who landed the commercial jetliner in the Hudson River in New York. The plane hit a flock of geese, causing the engine to fail. Captain Sullenberger seemed to miraculously land his plane in the Hudson River, and incredibly saved everyone onboard.

Everyone on that plane knew who to thank. They knew to thank the pilot who landed that plane safely in the river.

Now, let's imagine you're at 35,000 feet and one of the engines goes out. The pilot announces, "We're not sure what happened, but one of our engines is failing. But don't worry, we can still fly with three engines instead of four."

A few minutes later, boom, another engine goes out. The captain gets on the intercom again. He calmly states, "We lost another engine, but not to worry, we can still fly with two."

Boom, boom, the other two engines quit. The captain, with a little bit of panic in his voice, says, "We've lost all four engines. I'm not sure how this is going to play out, but get ready for a crash landing."

Then without any kind of explanation, boom, an engine starts up again. Then boom, another engine comes back to life.

Before you know it, all four engines are operating in their usual powerful modes. The pilot comes back on the intercom system. He says he is baffled as to why they quit and why they started up again.

Who do you thank then? Someone higher and greater than you. Someone or something wonder-ful.

Children know who to thank for putting candy in their stockings at Christmas. Who do you thank for putting two perfectly designed feet into yours?

When we lose the sense of wonder, we lose a sense of gratitude. Meaning becomes mangled in our lives.

We need to contemplate. We need to think about what's important in life, and about the things that make us wonder.

The second mindful practice to help us to think is to <u>resonate</u>.

Resonance is that quality of sound waves that when they begin to resonate, harmony occurs.

When we're in resonance, who we are outside aligns with who we are inside.

How aligned are your behaviors that are seen on the outside, to your core beliefs and values that drive them on the inside?

Are you someone of integrity? Do you have character that matters? Do you have a depth of who you are that expresses itself outwardly?

How aligned and resonant are you from the wave of who you are on the outside to the wave of who you are on the inside, and does it harmonize?

Resonance and harmony happen if we take time to think about what our values are.

Who it is that you are? What it is that you are most interested in?
What it is that you value more than anything else?

You don't get what you want. You get who you are.

You need to take time to resonate.

Examine your life to see if the internal and the external are aligned in
your lives, and if integrity and character are there.

Few people scratch the surface, much less exhaust the contemplation
and wonder of their own experience.

Take time to think.

Be ready not to be ready.

Make full use of the present.

Let go of what's going away.

Take time to think.

Take another look at your **Wheel of Resilience**.

See where you're focused. How well do you think? How well do you contemplate? How is your resonance? Examine in your life what we've covered so far. Discover where you stand on the **Wheel of Resilience**.

Resilience Skill 5: Live with the Long View (Be Hopeful)

The next step, after taking time to think, is to live with the long view.

Live with the long view.

Walker Percy, an American author, wrote a short story called *The Man on the Train.*

The man in his story is an extremely precise man.

This man lives by a schedule. He lives by the clock.

He lives by a plan that he carefully laid out where every single day is the same thing.

He gets up at the same exact time. He eats the same breakfast. He takes the same train, at the same exact same time every day. He works the same job that he has had every day of his working life. He leaves that job at the exact same time at the end of every day. He takes the same train home at the exact same time each day. He interacts with his family in the same manner, and eats dinner with them at the exact same time each evening.

The author says that there's something internally missing within him. There isn't a resonance, because how this man feels on the inside is so different from the orderly life that he lives on the outside. Other people see that he is disconnected. He's unhappy. Nothing matters to him. There seems to be no meaning for him. Life itself seems an agitation for him.

The story goes on with this man getting up at the same time, eating the same breakfast, and waiting for the same train that comes at the same time.

When one day, unexpectedly, he has a massive heart attack. Suddenly, there's something in his life for which he didn't plan.

Something big occurred in his life that isn't within the orderly life he planned. He finds his body worked on by people he has never met, in an ambulance that he has never before ridden in, en route to a hospital that he has never visited before.

As he's taken from the back of the ambulance on the gurney to the operating room, the author does a masterful job of describing what this man does.

As he was laying there on the gurney being whisked to the operating room, all he could focus and concentrate on was his own hand. He looked at it. He couldn't believe how amazing this appendage was. It was as if he'd never seen it before.

The translucence of the skin and how the fingernails grew, and did so every single day, and he'd unceremoniously clip them.

He can't believe the wonder of what's in his own hand. The five fingers and the palm. Why and how had he missed this wonderment?

The story goes on. The man has surgery and recovers well from it, but he is different.

He changes everything. He spends more time with his kids. He eases up on the hours he puts in at work. He makes massive changes so that he can live a fuller and complete life.

The author ends his story with a comparison to Rip Van Winkle waking up. The story of Rip Van Winkle, by Washington Irving, is about a man named Rip who goes to sleep for 20 years. When he wakes up two decades later, the world has changed dramatically. It's the same with this man in our story by Walker Percy.

It's as if our man had been sleeping most of his life and now, suddenly, he's woken up to what is wondrous in the world.

In other words, he has learned to live with the long view.

Things often make more sense when they're seen from up above in a sky box. It translates into investing in things that are worthy investments, like significance and perspective on life.

How significant is your life? How significant are the things that you do, and the decisions that you make?

You must invest in significance.

Consider the mechanical rabbit at every greyhound race track.

Every rabbit at every track is named Rusty. The greyhounds are enticed and motivated to run and to race when the mechanical rabbit is released. The dogs think they're on a hot pursuit in a hunt.

The announcer is always right when he says, "Here comes Rusty!" Vroom! That rabbit is seemingly running along the track. The dogs are freed from their pens to go after the rabbit. They're running, they're racing, they're barking and they can't wait, and then they're flying around the track. That's how the dogs are enticed to race.

Every once in a while, a greyhound will run so fast he'll grab the rabbit. That greyhound will never race again, because he knows he's been duped all this time. "It's a fake rabbit! It's not even real. What the heck am I doing wasting all this energy for a fake rabbit?"

How many fake rabbits do we have in our lives that we chase and pursue in so many different ways?

Stop chasing mechanical rabbits and invest yourself in what's real and what truly matters, and be significant.

Invest also in your perspective on life. To get a good idea of people's perspectives on life, look at the bumper stickers on their cars. The short, pithy statements of philosophy sum up what that particular person's philosophy or perspective is on life. If you have one, is it what you want to be known for?

A bumper sticker that I saw said, "There is no gravity; the earth sucks." That's a philosophy all right.

How about, "What if the hokey pokey really is what it's all about?" How depressing would that be?

What would your bumper sticker statement be? Have you created one? Have you thought enough about it so that when people look at you, they're able to recite it? If people ask you what you're all about, you're able to say, "This is it"?

The bumper sticker of a friend of mine states, "Live well by doing good." It's a great perspective on life.

My bumper sticker message is, "Re-imagine a hope-filled world." It's what gets me out of bed in the morning, and has me interact with my family and friends, and speak with audiences because I have this undercurrent running in me. I want everyone to re-imagine a hope filled world. That is my perspective on life.

I challenge you to create your bumper sticker statement. What would it say? Wrestle with it. Wrangle through it. Get it down to a covert operation statement that says "This is what I'm about. This is the undercurrent of everything I do. This is who I am."

Invest in the message you would promote on your own bumper sticker. It will help you live with a longer view that your life has a big 'Why' behind it. Knowing your Why gives you something deeper and grander to your life than simply getting up every morning, eating breakfast, going to work, and coming home from work. Involve your Why.

You need to invest in what's significant, but you also need to invest in your perspective, so that you can live with the long view. This is another way to be incredibly resilient in times of change.

Don't be afraid of failure, be afraid of succeeding at something that doesn't really matter.

On your **Wheel of Resilience** now, how hopeful are you? How hopeful is your perspective? How hopeful is your long view? Is there significance to your life? Have you come up with a bumper sticker statement? Do you know what's your big Why of life?

Mark these factors on your **Wheel of Resilience**.

Resilience Skill 6: Don't *Should* on Yourself (Be Balanced)

This next resilience skill allows you to engage with the marauders of change is *don't should on yourself.*

We're good at shoulding on ourselves. We poke the finger at our own chest all the time and we should ourselves: we should do this, we should do that, we should've, could've, would've. My neighbor, a good friend of mine who's a psychiatrist, says, "*Should* is one of the leading causes of most psychoses in the world. It's because we're living by shoulds all the time."

I should on myself. When my wife and I were first married, it was 1989. On the cover of Rolling Stone magazine was a picture of the Apple computer icon falling apart, and it had as its title, "The fall of an American icon." Apple was bankrupt. The company was going nowhere. I loved Macs from their beginning.

On seeing that cover, I remember telling my wife, "You know what, I should invest. I really should, because I don't think they're going away. I think Apple will turn around. I think Apple will stay." At that time, the stock was $5 to $6 a share. And now, it's several hundred dollars per share.

My son, who knows our story, repeatedly calculates what might have been. "Dad, if you bought this many shares at $5 a share, you know how rich we'd be right now?"

I should have bought Apple stock, but I didn't. I could say should should should should should should the rest of my life, and it's not going to get me anywhere.

Don't should on yourself. To make sure you don't, you need to take some <u>preventative measures</u>.

The first preventative measure is to monitor your *self-talk*. We each have a running dialogue in our brains, telling us this and telling us that about ourselves. Our self-talk is so often derogatory to ourselves. We would never talk that way to anybody else. But we do speak that way to ourselves, and it's not a good way to go.

What's your explanatory style? The event happens, the consequence happens, what happens in your thought processes in between?

My dad provides a classic example of a poor explanatory style. For example, when he's on vacation, if he can't find his sunglasses, his mantra becomes "The day is shot. The whole day is shot. Can't find my sunglasses, might as well just stay home."

Dad, holy cow. That's an explanatory style and it's not a very good one. What is your explanatory style? Do you tend to look at things more from a positive or from a negative point of view?

On Winnie the Pooh shows, Eeyore's theme is "Life is bad. I'm not going to build any shelter. I'm just going to get wet anyway."

Then there's Tigger's mantra. "I'm a Tigger, that's what Tigger's do best," as he's bouncing around like crazy.

When it comes to your self-esteem, are you more Eeyore, or are you more Tigger?

Neither mantra is the best. You need to find out where you are in the spectrum. Be you, actual size. Be you actual size, warts and all. Once you come to grips with that, that's a wonderful place to be, and you'll stop shoulding on yourself, and you'll become more resilient. The paradox of change is that change occurs when one becomes what he is, not when he tries to become what he is not.

Take preventative measures to not should on yourself. First, monitor your self-talk. Then regulate your self-esteem.

I worked with a client who was a successful businessman in Virginia, who requested my help with a presentation that he was to give. He started a collection agency years ago. His employee turnover rate in the collection agency is about 2%. That low of a figure is rare. Employee turnover rates in collection agencies are extremely high because who wants to spend their time begging for money and throttling people to get money out of them? His turnover rate is 2%.

He believes the reason is because he has helped his employees with their self-esteem. They see themselves as more than collection agents, more than thugs that are getting money out of others. Now, he wants to go on the road giving presentations and help other business people with the importance of healthy and proper self-esteem for employees, and indeed everyone.

On the **Wheel of Resilience**, how balanced are you in your thought processes? How truthful are you being with yourself? How is the self-talk between negative and positive? How's your self-esteem? How balanced are you in your view of yourself?

Mark your **Wheel of Resilience** to see where you're at on these factors.

Be ready not to be ready. Make full use of the present. Let go of what's going away. Take time to think. Live with the long view. Don't should on yourself.

Resilience Skill 7: Don't Go It Alone

(Be Connected)

Another important resilience skill to engage the marauders of change is don't go it alone.

Don't go it alone.

I found a revealing letter to an insurance agency from a bricklayer. In the letter, he's trying to get a premium and get paid for the injuries that he sustained.

This is the bricklayer's explanation to the insurance company.

"Dear sir. I am writing in response to your request for additional information for my insurance claim. In block number three of the accident claim form, I wrote, 'Trying to do the job alone' as the cause of my accident. You said in your letter that I should explain that statement more fully. I believe the following details will be sufficient.

"I am a bricklayer by trade. On the date of the accident, I was working alone on the roof of a new six story building. When I completed my work, I discovered that I had about 500 pounds of bricks left over. Rather than carrying the bricks down by hand, I decided to lower them in a barrel by using a pulley, which was attached to the side of the building at the sixth floor level. Securing the rope at ground level, I went up to the roof, swung the barrel out, and loaded the bricks into it. Then I went back down to the ground and untied the rope, holding it tightly to ensure a slow descent of the 500 pounds of bricks.

"You will note in block number 22 of the claim form that my weight is 150 pounds. Due to my surprise at being jerked off the ground so suddenly, I lost my presence of mind and forgot to let go of the rope. Needless to say, I proceeded up the side of the building at a very rapid rate of speed. In the vicinity of the third floor, I met the barrel coming down, which explains my fractured skull and collarbone.

"Slowed only slightly, I continued my rapid ascent, not stopping until the fingers of my right hand were two knuckles deep into the pulley. By this time, I had regained my presence of mind and was able to hold

74

tightly to the rope in spite of my pain. At approximately the same time however, the barrel of bricks hit the ground and the bottom fell out of the barrel. Devoid of the weight of the bricks, the barrel then weighed approximately 50 pounds.

"I refer you again to the information in block number 22 regarding my weight. As you might imagine, I began a rapid descent down the side of the building, and in the vicinity of the third floor, I met the barrel coming up, which accounts for the two fractured ankles and the lacerations of my legs and lower body. This second encounter with the barrel slowed me enough to lessen my injuries when I fell into the pile of bricks, and fortunately, only three vertebrae were cracked.

"I am sorry to report however as I lay there on the bricks in pain, unable to stand and watching the empty barrel six stories above me, I again lost my presence of mind and let go of the rope. The empty barrel weighed more than the rope so it proceeded at a rapid descent down the side of the building, landing on and breaking both of my legs.

"I hope I have furnished enough information that is sufficient enough to explain that trying to do the job alone was the stated cause of the accident."

Things don't work out very well if we do things alone. We live in a culture that exemplifies the self-made billionaire. Our culture's attitude is "I don't need anybody. I don't need this help or that help."

You can't be resilient if you go it alone. The way that you don't go it alone is you need to rely on your relational resources. One relational resource, and this is new in human history, is all the social networks that technology has provided.

You may remember the game that was happening a few years back called Six Degrees of Kevin Bacon. Basically, what that means is that between you and Kevin Bacon are only five other people, and if you discovered who those five people were, you yourself could meet Kevin Bacon.

The concept originated from a sociology test in the 1960s where a man determined that we are six degrees removed from anybody else on the planet. Given our social networks, however, with Facebook, Twitter, LinkedIn and all the rest, we are now three degrees separated from anyone else on the planet.

When I was reading that statistic to my wife, we figured out that we are three degrees removed from Barack Obama in two different ways. Three degrees.

That means between you and anyone else on the entire planet, are two other people. Find out who those two other people are, and you will have the introduction you want or need.

To not go it alone, you can rely on your social networks. Social networks are a great way to not go it alone in business, too. Let people know you're looking for work or that you have a new product available. You've made a fantastic product. Maybe it's a candle and it smells great. Let people know about it. Social networks are a great way to not go it alone.

Another relational resource to rely on to not go it alone are your intimate bonds. Intimate bonds with the few people that, for the most part, you're fully vulnerable and fully available with. They're fully vulnerable and fully available for you.

I've learned over time to rely on my intimate bonds to not go it alone. Since age 16, I've struggled with bipolar depression. Bone jarring depression. It's something that I have to manage every single day of my life.

When I was in college, I had no idea what it was, really. No one did. My roommate, my best friend, could tell when I was starting to spiral down into that place of darkness. He learned what the signs were. When he noticed them appearing again, he would get me up off the couch or out of my bed and say, "We're going for a walk." It wasn't just any walk.

On those walks, what he provided for me were swisher sweets cigars. If you don't know swisher sweets cigars, they're shorter, thin, and they have a flavored tip on the end. We would walk around the neighborhood smoking swisher sweets cigars, and it did more for me in my depression than almost anything else. I love him to this day for that.

Ask yourself, who are your swisher sweets? Who are you being a swisher sweet for?

You need to have intimate bonds in your life. We need to have swisher sweets in our lives who help us get out of our funk, to help us have a different perspective on life, to help us let go of what's going away, to help us make full use of the present, to help us do all these things that make us more resilient. Who or what are your swisher sweets?

We are a knot into which relationships are tied. How connected are you? How connected do you feel?

Mark where you're at with your relational resources on your **Wheel of Resilience**.

Some of the resilience skills we've covered so far are being open, committed, adventurous, focused, hopeful, balanced, and connected. Another great resilience skill we need is to learn to yuck it up.

Resilience Skill 8: Yuck It Up

(Be Jovial)

We need to laugh a little bit.

Some interesting learnings about humor and resilience came from the old The Daily Show with Jon Stewart. It was a wildly popular show because it made hard news palatable by using satire and humor. Humor is the most advanced defense mechanism that we have in dealing with the big issues of the world.

One study concluded that people who watched The Daily Show were more up to date on world events than those who watched the network news shows. More people got their news from The Daily Show than from the network news shows, and that illustrates the power of humor and satire in our lives.

Another study about humor was conducted by Laugh Lab. A guy named Dick Winehouse traveled around the globe, with the goal of finding the funniest joke in the entire world. He found three jokes that came to the top of the list.

The funniest joke in the entire world, according to his research, is the following joke.

Two men were on a hunting trip and one of the men suddenly fell over. His eyes were glazed and he didn't seem to be breathing. His partner got on his cellphone and called 911 and said, "I think my partner is dead." The 911 operator said, "Okay, calm down, the first thing we need to do is make sure he's dead." A couple seconds later, a gunshot fires out. The friend gets back on the phone, "Okay, now what?"

That was the joke deemed the world's funniest by Mr. Winehouse.

The second funniest joke in the world was about Sherlock Holmes and Watson. They went camping and pitched their tent. In the middle of the night, Sherlock woke up and realized he could see the stars. He woke up Watson and said, "What do you see up there, Watson?"

Watson said, "I see thousands and thousands of stars in the darkness of this night."

"What can you deduce from that, Watson?" asked Sherlock.

Watson replied, "We're not alone, I don't think. With all those stars, there's got to be other galaxies, there's got to be other planets, there's got to be more intelligent life."

Sherlock said, "No, someone stole our tent."

That was Winehouse's second funniest joke in the world.

Some of you might say, "Those aren't very funny," but that's what Dick Winehouse decided.

The third funniest joke is more popular in the United Kingdom than in the United States. It goes like this.

A woman got on a bus with her baby. The bus driver said, "That's the ugliest baby I have ever seen."

The mother, fuming while walking to the back of the bus, said, "I can't believe that this bus driver insulted me more than I could ever say."

The passenger guy next to her says, "You ought to go back up and talk to him. I'll hold your monkey while you do."

Yuck it up to build resilience.

Yucking it up and laughing taps into a <u>couple benefits</u>. The first one is that it helps keep us sane. Jimmy Buffet, that great American musician and sometimes philosopher, said that if we all couldn't laugh, we would all go insane. It is so true

More often than not, we're not laughing ha ha, as much as laughing aha.

Humor is the heart sweating. It's a way to release tension. It's a way to keep us all sane.

Applebee's restaurants figured out a good use of humor some years ago. You could go to Applebee's and get inflatable employees. Then you could set them in your office space, go to lunch at Applebee's and stay for a couple hours because your boss would be fooled.

We need more frivolity in the workplace. If you talk to millennials, or if you talk to Xers, they learned their ABCs and 123s because they watched it from the Electric Company or Sesame Street. Instead of teachers in the front of the room, they had Big Bird and Ernie. They translated that to the workplace, and they wanted their work to be a little frivolous, to have a little bit of fun and a little bit of joy.

It's a good, good thing. In fact, the top companies, 90% of them say one of the key reasons for their success is they have a sense of humor, they allow laughter in the workplace.

Yuck it up. It keeps us sane, and secondly, it also helps keep us healthy.

Humor is the difference between running on adrenaline and running on endorphins. Adrenaline is high alert, where stress comes in. Adrenaline is what keeps us from calming ourselves down.

Endorphins are what make us feel good. Endorphins are those chemicals that laughter releases that give us a calming effect. They help give us perspective.

Yuck it up. The more you find out about the world, the more opportunities there are to laugh. How jovial are you? Mark it on your **Wheel of Resilience**.

How well are you able to laugh? Not only at yourself, but at the world around you, and do it in a way that's healthy, that keeps you sane and that helps keep you physically healthy. How jovial are you?

Resilience Skill 9: Practice Bricolage (Be Adaptable)

The last skill we need for resilience to help us engage the marauders of change is to practice bricolage.

On April 11, 1970, the Apollo 13 mission was sent into space. It was going to be the third mission to the moon, when an oxygen tank blew, and the astronauts were stuck in between the earth and the moon.

You may have seen the movie, Apollo 13, and you remember they did not know how they were going to get back to earth. They were, for the most part, crippled up there. The engineers of NASA had to do what they could do to bring them back from space.

Complicating the situation was that the filtration system broke. That system was designed to take the deadly carbon dioxide out of the air that came from the astronauts' breath. Not only were they mechanically stuck in space, but they were slowly suffocating to death.

The NASA engineers back on earth had to figure out how to get the broken filter going again or how to create a filter that would take the carbon dioxide out. But in doing so. they had a challenge. The engineers couldn't build it out of items that they had on hand there on earth, they had to build it using only what the Apollo 13 spacecraft crew had on board.

Using a tube sock, and using plastic and cardboard from flight manuals, and other items the astronauts had at their disposal, the engineers created and built the filtration system that ended up saving the astronauts' lives. Those engineers at NASA practiced bricolage.

Bricolage is an obscure word that means you make the most of whatever resources you have on hand.

You think not outside the box. Instead, you think wildly inside the box. You take things that are available to you and reconstitute them in new ways. You make things work. Practicing bricolage is making great use of whatever resources you have on hand.

Think about the box that you are in. Think about the resources that you have. We have certain budgets. We have to work within those confines of the budgets. We have certain gifts and talents, we have to work within those gifts and those talents.

The things of our lives, physically, monetarily or otherwise, are all limited. Using and practicing bricolage is making the most of those things that we have for the benefit of ourselves and for others.

To be resilient, we need to practice bricolage, by using some <u>techniques of improvisation</u>.

One technique is accepting the situation. Improv rolls in the moment. Improvisational actors accept the situation.

A classic improv example is having an idea for a situation thrown at the improve actors from the audience, and the improv actors must work with the suggested situation within the confines of where they are at.

Not only do they accept the situation, another technique is they have a way of moving the scene forward. They work from their gut and from instinct.

If you become more improvisational, the more you're able to practice bricolage because you accept the situation as it is, and work within its confines to move it forward.

Our NASA engineers improvised when carbon dioxide was in the air, and there was no filtration system to remove it. They had to find the fix.

That was their situation. They accepted the situation, and did what they could with their work to move the scene forward. That is practicing bricolage.

Face your reality first, and then engage it.

How well can you use the F word in your life every day? Flexibility.

How flexible are you when things in life come your way?

On the **Wheel of Resilience**, how adaptable are you?

Summary

Resilience predicts our future. The Harvard Business Review said that more than experience, more than knowledge, resilience was the number one indicator for success or failure in an organization.

I would say more than that, resilience is also the number one indicator of how well we cope and how well we do in the changes that are going on in our lives.

We need to be ready not to be ready. We need to make full use the present. We need to let go of what's going away. We need to take time to think, we need to live with the long view. We shouldn't should on ourselves. Don't go it alone. Yuck it up. Practice bricolage.

It might mean you need to find a new beach. I listened to an interview on National Public Radio after Hurricane Katrina happened. The interviewers were talking to an engineer. All around was wreckage from Hurricane Katrina. It was terrible and miserable, and things were not where they should be, like cars were on top of houses.

The interviewer asked this engineer, "With all the wreckage around here, what are you hoping to find?"

The engineer gave an answer that surprised me. "I'm going to find a new beach."

Amid the wreckage of Hurricane Katrina, the engineer's perspective was that his mission was to find a new beach.

That should be the mission of each of us as we go through life. As things get tough and changes get to be a little bit overwhelming, we need to have the desire to find a new beach.

Resilience is your way to find a new beach.

With resilience we shape new perceptions, invite new resources, and embrace new directions.

Every organization needs to do those things. Every life needs to do those things. Every person needs to do those things. Every family needs to do those things

Resilience is the number one indicator of how well we're going to do in the changes that are coming our way.

Changes are coming at us fast and furious.

How well will your skills in resilience meet and master them?

THE WHEEL OF RESILIENCE

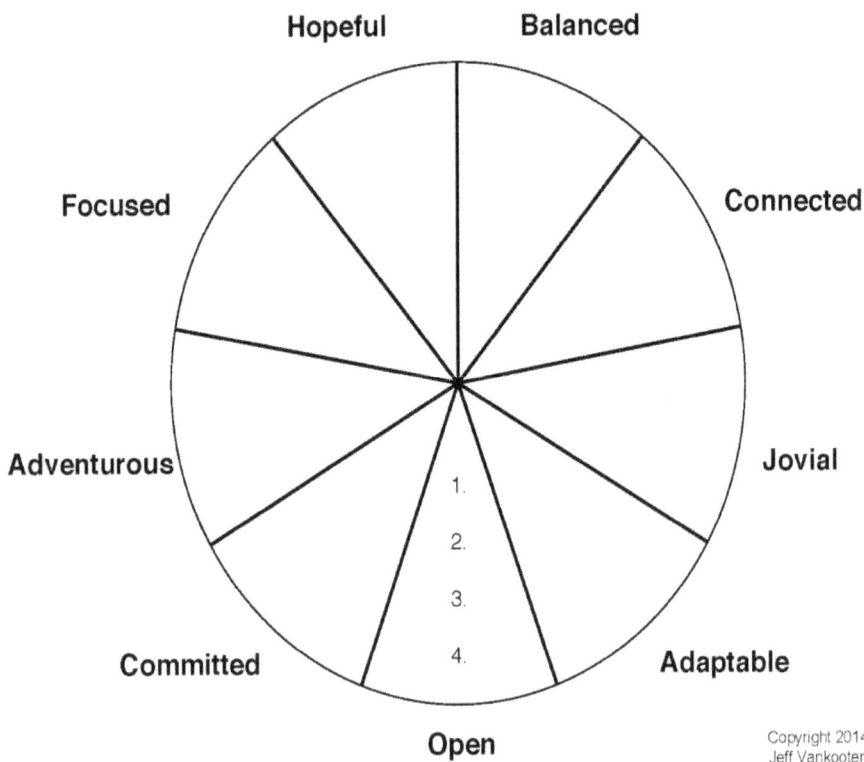

Hopeful

Balanced

Focused

Connected

Adventurous

Jovial

1.
2.
3.
4.

Committed

Adaptable

Open